One Day,
I Found Tennis

One Day,
I Found Tennis

Diane M. Griffin

iUniverse, Inc.
New York Lincoln Shanghai

One Day, I Found Tennis

iUniverse books may be ordered through booksellers or by contacting:

iUniverse
2021 Pine Lake Road, Suite 100
Lincoln, NE 68512
www.iuniverse.com
1-800-Authors (1-800-288-4677)

The views expressed in this work are solely those of the author and do not necessarily reflect the views of the publisher, and the publisher hereby disclaims any responsibility for them.

ISBN: 978-0-595-43647-7 (pbk)
ISBN: 978-0-595-87974-8 (ebk)

Printed in the United States of America

For Mrs. Lucinda T. Griffin
My Mother

Contents

Acknowledgement

A huge "Thank you" to:

God, for "manna," a little bit of inspiration every day, which is all I needed.

My mother, Mrs. Lucinda T. Griffin, who is my inspiration.

The man who brought me to the game of tennis.

My brother, for his encouragement.

The Chicago businessman.

Preface

What's a girl to do, when she knows there's got to be a better way to enjoy a workout? The answer could be, "just wait." That's what I did, and "One day, I Found Tennis." The door to an incredible new world opened for me, and life just keeps getting better. I found in tennis, something more than just the game.

Early morning tennis always makes me feel like a winner, especially outside in invigorating breezes of fresh air and sunshine. Then, there's tennis under lights! Yes! A friendly game of strategic, athletic, competitive tennis under the beauty of a sunset, is an awesome experience. It's fun, relaxing, and good for the soul. You can leave with your racket in one hand, and tennis balls in the other, feeling as if you won the Tennis U.S. Open.

And, just watching adults "play" recreational tennis, against opponents who are sometimes twice beneath their age, subtlety states tennis must be some type of medicine for anti-aging, as well as, for any and all physical and physiological ills. It's for all these reasons, and more, that since the day I found tennis, I can't fathom living without it.

Introduction

This personal memoir of my view of the world of tennis reflects my passion, as well as, my delight for this incredible recreational sport. Here are my first experiences of the game, and how my life flourished when I met others who play the game of tennis.

The arrangement is an introductory tennis love story about me, a woman who triumphs over boring, routine exercise. This particular story is about how I found tennis, and why I stuck with the game. Can you find love on the tennis court? Perhaps!

Then, what follows are mini stories about champions, who each followed their heart to tennis. The Real Meaning of Tennis, sums up my stance about the game of tennis. Psychological and Physical Reasons/ Advantages of Playing Tennis, are sections of a list of why anyone, at any age, might be motivated to play tennis. Check it out! It's motivational. Lastly, Poems, is a section of lyrical verses which express my encounters, my amusements, as well as my anticipations for the future of the game.

Let me share with you, why tennis "rocks" in my life.

The Day The Door Opened

There are moments during a person's lifetime when something happens which can alter the course of their life. We may meet someone, go somewhere, or do something we may have never done before. These precise moments are the possibilities, which can guide us to where we're supposed to go and what we're supposed to do with our lives.

God was in His glory that day. Assortments of colorful flowers, lush green grass and birds whistling pleasant melodies in the air ensured me Fall was in full season. It was a Saturday afternoon. After a long bike ride from Navy Pier, I felt relaxed, and pleased to be enjoying my weekend, after having wrestled through a long week of busy hustle and bustle.

I've always enjoyed bike riding. However, the adventurous, energetic inner me, wanted something more exciting. I had felt this way for quite some time, while I hung in there with boring workouts in gyms. I had exhausted myself with jogging and aerobics, and even gotten desperate enough to try roller blading. Yes, roller blading! It didn't take me long though, to trade in my roller blades ... not for the price I paid for them. I settled for the small price of $8, with the advantage of walking away without having lost any of my teeth or major body parts.

Yes, nature seemed to be showing off this day. It was a fabulously pleasant, sunny, September afternoon. So pleasant, I detoured from the bike path into Harold Washington Park. Harold Washington Park is a cozy park, set in Chicago's Hyde Park community. There, I felt a generous breeze from Lake Michigan, which seem to kiss the park with relief from an unseasonably warm day. I happened to capture, slightly above the park, a flock of white Sea birds.

Gliding my bike over towards the children's playground, I heard sounds of gaiety. Nearing home, I approached the parkway, where a man opened the door of the outdoor tennis court gate, and stepped out of the tennis courts.

This day, and meeting him, would lead me on my path to a life with the game of the tennis.

God Is Always In Control

We gravitated toward each other like magnets, when our eyes first met. Then, he waved to me to ride my bike over to where he was, as he carefully shut the door of the gate of the tennis court behind him. A tennis racket was strapped across his right shoulder.

Nearing toward him, I wondered if I was saying hello to an old friend. His features resembled those of one of my old school mates. He was unshaven and grubby, yet, I couldn't help concede the truth, he was exceptionally good looking. We even greeted each other as if we had been acquainted before.

"You're not in a hurry," he called out to me with a warm and inviting smile. Gleaming with the color of hazel, his eyes cast a look of sincerity when he smiled. His eyes seem to speak to me with a language all their own, which only my heart could understand. He had an air of charm. And, he was right; I wasn't in a hurry.

His smile seemed to be begging me to speak, so I stopped, rested my bike, then promptly used the tennis racket as a conversation piece. I stated the obvious, "How's your game?"

"Pretty good." He said, while looking at my bike.

"Nice ride?" He stated.

"Most definitely!" I said confidently. "I just rode to Navy Pier and back."

We proceeded to get acquainted with our small talk, as slowly, I was becoming more impressed, with his striking, athletic looks. My imagination wondered, as I began to speculate as to whether or not he had a job, with a good health care plan, and owned a Bible with highlighted verses. Then, I stopped myself, "Too soon to be thinking so far ahead!" I thought.

I felt as if I were reading his lips, as slowly, he said, "Do you mind if I call you sometime?"

"Oh, I live down the street. If you play here often, I'll see you around." I said.

Then, I gripped my bike, and hopped on, hoping this would convince him not to ask me again.

"Hold on a minute, he insisted, and I'll find a pen.

Racket To Riches

Of course, if I were going to hang out with him, I would have to know how to play tennis. Consequently, days later, I found myself heading to the storage room of the building I live in, to bring my old tennis racket out of storage. Seeing my old racket again brought back memories of years ago when I bought it:

"OK," I told the man at the sports store, I'll take these three cute little skirts, three pairs of socks, three tee shirts to match, and this fabulous pair of tennis shoes."

"It's a 'must' to look good on the tennis court." He said.

"Absolutely!" I agreed.

"Will you be needing anything else?" He asked.

"Oh yes, of course," I said, looking up at the row of tennis rackets hanging on a wall.

"Yes?" He spoke politely.

"There will be one more thing. I'll be needing a tennis racket!"

"Of course!" He replied.

I, of course, had no idea of what type of racket I needed, or in fact, whether or not the type of racket I used had any effect on the way I played the game. I was an absolute novice to the sport.

"Any particular type?" He asked.

"Oh, any old racket will do." I replied.

I had taken more time choosing my outfits than on choosing the most important thing, my racket! My weapon! My sword of destruction!

So, now, as I stood here in the storage room, my hindsight was clear.

"I should have gotten a better racket." I thought.

Holding this racket in my hand, looking at it from a distance, I caught myself when I made the expression on my face of "despair." I looked at the racket as if it were something foreign. I blew the dust off of the racket, and, I resolved that it wasn't much, but it was all I had. I would have to use what I had and make it work for me.

Court One

The first time he took me to the court to learn to play tennis, I was amazed at how many luxury, antique cars, custom-made motor cycles, and motor bikes lined the driveway to the tennis courts. 'Prosperity,' spoke out loudly and clearly.

We stepped onto Court One, where the atmosphere is always welcoming and friendly. People from all walks of life were there that day, with fascinating, stimulating conversation about anything from politics to religion. Conversations were astoundingly forthcoming, and friendly. The people there seemed to be glad they were in a place where they didn't have to feel inhibited, nor did they have to be careful about voicing an opinion. Seated on benches, seemingly waiting for the opportunity to get a game, were attractive, intelligent-looking, healthy-looking men and women, laughing and talking. They were a diverse, uninhibited group who made the game of tennis associated with an energetic and successful lifestyle. They were not misleading. When they each got up to play tennis, they were hard hitting, strategizing competitors. They had a certain appeal. Here I was, standing in the mist of where I knew would become one of my favorite places.

We played next to Court One. I wasn't ready for Court One. Court One was a place with a level playing field. No hierarchies ... strictly competitive tennis. On Court One, every point you got, you earned. Court One was unofficially reserved for the better players who brought their best game. And, if you were to look closely enough in their eyes, you'd find, they all had one thing in common, the eye of the tiger. They had a hungry look of competitiveness to win.

When the man I met guided me to an empty court, my immediate challenge, was to simply concentrate on getting the ball to go over the other side of the net. Initially, when I swung at ball, my aim was to just keep from hitting the ball in Court One, next to us. After all, I was in the company of seasoned players; I didn't need to get their feathers ruffled.

I played well for a beginner, as I eagerly swung at the ball, attentively holding the racket just the way he taught me. Lesson number one was, "Keep your eyes on the ball. Don't take your eyes off for a millisecond!" He would exclaim. "Get that racket back, and follow all the way through."

The first lessons he taught, I would need to always remember whenever I played tennis. Later, I would begin learning more beginning fundamentals of the game.

Though this was my first time on the court, the bending to pick up the balls, and the stretching to reach and hit the balls, helped my muscles feel tighter. I felt lean, fit, and athletic. Any awkwardness I felt initially faded, as I began to blend in socially with the other players. After my first lesson, I was already hooked. Few workouts compared to this! Ironically, after all of that running and starting and stopping, I actually felt more energetic! I was getting more exercise than ever, having more fun than in my routine workouts at the gym, and burning more calories!

Determined to get in at least three days of practice a week, I allowed the man who introduced himself to me on that beautifully sunny day in September, to become my constant companion. Or, was my constant companion becoming my favorite tennis partner? In any case, we were connecting … bonding like two peas in a pod. After all, he was much more experienced than I. So, I appreciated his patience, and how he consistently helped and encouraged me. It meant a lot to me. He showed no sign of embarrassment to be with me, even though I was a novice to the game of tennis.

Every time we'd go to Court One together, was better than the last. We'd spend most evenings playing tennis until the sun went down. When it got so dark so that we couldn't play, we always shared leisurely walks home. Sometimes, I'd lean on his shoulder, while we both gulped Gatorade to quench our thirsts. And, we'd talk about how I might be better the next time we returned to the tennis court. I always got a kick out of it whenever he'd say, "someday, you'll be *better* than me." Talk about motivation!

Consequently, tennis was always at the top of my list of things to do. We saw quite a lot of each other, and entertained each other in just about everything we did socially. We attended church, outdoor jazz and blues festivals, the Air and Water show, barbeques, parties, and, of course, always included, was lots of tennis.

He and I almost lived at Court One. We played tennis there after work. We played tennis there on Saturday mornings, and we played tennis there on Sunday evenings. Any day and any time was always a good day and time for tennis. Slowly, I was falling spellbound by his handsome looks and gentlemanly manners, while I was being captured by the game of tennis.

Just Us, Just Tennis

After more dates on the court, the game was giving me more than I ever expected a sport to offer. I was looking and feeling better. The man who led me to tennis was charming, and I laughed so much with him, that before I knew it, we were entertaining each other as much as possible. I was becoming as enthusiastic about him being around, as I was about tennis. Everything I experienced, I wanted him to experience, too. Every song, which touched my heart, I wanted to touch his, too. Everything I read, I wanted him to know about, too. And, every time I stepped on the court to play tennis, I thought about him, and I wanted him to be there, too. I always felt fortunate to have him as a partner. And, it was clear to me why it was seldom to hear anyone speak of tennis and not include the word "fun."

On occasion, after we'd played a few matches, we'd stroll over to the Point, a coveted place, near the shore of Lake Michigan, where the rocks form a peak. We'd sit on the gigantic rocks near the shore, as we watched countless waves roll in and splash the shore. Continually critiquing our games, we were physically exhausted, yet, we were alive and refreshed within. Both of us seemed to be possessed with a renewed, inner sense of peace, invigoration and exalted self-esteem, which lasted long after we left the court.

As the sun would set softly behind us, Chicago's skyline seemed to boast in the far distance, as we'd allow the embodiment of it all to wash away everything else but the happiness we felt wrapped up in. As we engaged each other with visions of what we looked forward to in the future, the sky would get too dark for us to see each other. Then, we'd head home. Slowly, reluctantly we'd leave the day behind, eagerly looking forward to the next day, together. It was a season to treasure. Just us. Just tennis.

Tennis Pays!

My first winter of tennis, after hanging in there through injures, costly lessons and court time, someone in one my tennis classes at the Tennis and Racket Club mentioned a 7:00 a.m. summer tennis class to me. "7:00 a.m.!" I thought. Frankly, even being the tennis fan that I am, I thought 7:00 a.m. was going a little over the top! What's worse? The class was on Saturdays! Nevertheless, I accepted the challenge. I got more than I bargained for and began to welcome early summer Saturday mornings.

Turned out, no pep talks or motivational speeches were needed. After I attended the first class, I was again, "hooked." I'd race eagerly to reconnect myself with the game of tennis after a long week. Beams of sunshine through the trees led me down a long path to a quaint set of tennis courts, set away in a somewhat remote area of a community park. Birds chirping and whistling atop dew covered leaves on tall trees, and the fresh morning air, were a delight to me. Often, when I got there, people were already there, stretching and doing warm ups. As the morning would advance, the sun would kiss my skin, pealing away any pressures of life.

It was at this class where I met a handsome Chicago businessman. His reason for joining the class was just to brush up his game. He was way past the beginning stages of tennis. The handsome Chicago businessman had played tennis for many years, and he looked as if he fit the same category of those players I first saw at Court One, where I was introduced to the game. He was debonair, physically fit, successful, and, he had game.

I blushed when he asked, "Does your boyfriend know you're out playing tennis looking so pretty, this early in the morning?" I thought about what he said for a moment. Then, without any conscience at all, I felt ready to admit something, not to him, yet, rather to myself.

The relationship I had with the man who introduced me to tennis was stronger than some, and had lasted longer than most. I had even imagined him as ideal. Yet, deep down inside of me, in my spirit, I had to come to terms with the truth. I knew our relationship was not meant to last forever. Any bewilderment I had, however, led to a happy ending. I had tennis. And, the desire to play and excel was now rooted inside of me.

I cannot say it was a coincidence that I met that man on that beautiful Fall day. For, it was that day, when God used him to begin to unfold for me, a new lifestyle in the game of tennis. Little things about the game of tennis, which he taught me, opened up a whole new exhilarating world for me and prepared me to meet new exciting people!

They say, every relationship is not meant to last; yet perhaps used to teach us something. And, hopefully we emerge from the relationship a better person as we move on through life. He made learning to play tennis, effortless and blissful for me. He was the man God used to usher me to the game, that day I found tennis. Without warning, my heart surrendered to a game, which would accessorize and impact my life.

Without him, I would have missed the sunny days and moonlit nights we shared romping barefoot in the sand on the beach, dipping our feet in the cool water of Lake Michigan. I would have missed our picnics on summer days. I would have missed tennis after dark for the first time on lighted courts. I would have missed our slow dances to Motown music with sips of champagne out of long stem glasses on my birthday. I would have missed watching the U.S. Open Finals for the first time with him. And, I would have missed his strong hand to hold for no reason at all.

In the meantime, the day the handsome Chicago businessman asked me to dinner, I accepted. And, I continue to accept every time since then, whenever he asks me. Can a tennis romance survive? Who knows? Anyway, I'm headed towards discovering a lifetime of tennis, maybe with him!

Each year, after squeezing all I can out of Indian summer, when Fall tries to disguise itself, yet, I know Fall is on it's way. When the Chicago Hawk makes its attempt to settle in for the winter, I vow to myself, "next summer, I'll come out and be a better player than I ever was before." When Chicago winters, bring softly falling snowflakes, chilly winds, and icicles which are enough to make a person forget lovely summers, I remember anyway. Even though outside tennis courts are lifeless and bare,

I reminisce, at my indulgence about visions of full tennis courts, which once lit up with active, vibrant, spirited people in the gleam of radiance and fun. And, slowly, yet reluctantly, it becomes a little easier to say good by to those Saturday and Sunday afternoons and evenings at Court One, at Harold Washington Park tennis courts.

Remnants of memories of the day tennis entered my life reoccur whenever I pass by those tennis courts. I recall the day my life was pleasantly introduced to the discovery of the game of tennis. Often, when I step on any tennis court, I revisit how this all started for me, and I think of him. I shall always remember him, and take with me, memories of how he lead my heart to discover this passion for tennis.

> -*"What though the radiance which was once so bright, is now forever taken from my sight.—Though nothing can bring back the hour of splendor in the grass, of glory in the flower, We will grieve not, but rather find strength in what remains behind." Odes of Imitations of Immortality. Henry Wadsworth Longfellow (1770–1850)*

Follow Your Heart To Tennis

If you've been gazing from outside of tennis courts as you walk by, with a silent desire to play, go ahead and let your heart lead the way for you. You'll be in good company.

- Tennis inspired an ordinary Black man, who had an extraordinary dream, to tutor his daughters in the game of tennis. With nothing more than a passion and admiration for the game of tennis, and aspiration, even before they were born, he dreamed of his daughters as successful tennis players. Imagine he and his daughters, playing with shabby rackets and nearly washed out balls, hitting against walls and playing on pot-holed courts in violence-riddled Compton, Los Angeles. His first three daughters didn't fit that destiny, but Venus and Serena took to the game immediately. The two Williams sisters, who began playing tennis at a very early age, attained the very height of tennis success, individually and collectively, reaching the pinnacle of the sport of tennis and they have garnered respect and admiration of tennis greats, as well as, millions of fans worldwide.

- Arthur Ashe left a remarkable tennis legacy. He cultivated his talent and passion for the sport of tennis despite segregation and spearheaded a color barrier to become the first African-American man to win Wimbledon, tennis' most coveted trophy, in 1975 and penetrate segregation in the world of tennis. Tennis began as a sport predominantly of the English speaking world. A game, once segregated by race and class, and played only by the elite, tennis, which originated in 12th Century France, was played by French aristocrats and eventually became dominated by players in the United States, Britain and Australia. Enduring racism on and off the tennis court, Arthur Ashe was blocked from competing nationally in tennis, yet, eventually broke color barriers, advanced history, and impacted social change.

- Althea Gibson was born on August 25, 1927, during a time when Black people were banned from public tennis courts in South Carolina. She moved with her family to New York City, to Harlem, where she developed an interest in tennis. In time, she quit high school, not because of tennis, but because she didn't like classes. Nonetheless, she attracted the attention of two tennis-playing doctors, Hubert Eaton of North Carolina and Robert W. Johnson of Virginia, who were both active in the tennis community in 1946. Each doctor took her into his family. Dr. Eaton during the school year, and in the summer, Robert W. Johnson, a wealthy doctor, who gave her the opportunity to play tennis on his private court. Althea Gibson, who was from a poor family, used this second opportunity in life. She not only graduated from high school in 1949; she followed her natural passion for tennis, which lead her to become the first African American woman to break the color barrier in professional female tennis. Though, still unwelcome in some tennis clubs where important tournaments were played, she yet, made history by becoming the first African-American who would go on to win Wimbledon in 1957 and 1958. Then, she went on to become ranked number one in the United States and the world. She won a total of 11 Grand Slam events before she was inducted into the International Hall of Fame and the International Women's Sports Hall of Fame.

- The game of tennis, urged Martina Navratilova, to leave behind her family and home. Having the courage to decide not to live in the Czech Republic, a country with a repressed regime, she moved to the United States to pursue her passion, tennis. She eventually became a United States citizen. As a child, her stepfather told her, "one day, you'll become champion at Wimbledon." Her first great achievement was when she won Wimbledon in 1978, and she continued to win major professional accomplishments competitively, even as she neared the age of 50, when she retired from professional play.

- James Blake, another African-American in the professional game of tennis, followed his heart and fought his way back to the game of tennis. After colliding into a tennis net post and suffering a broken neck, he recovered from this freak accident and made an amazing come back He was then faced with the death of his father, and a viral infection which left him with diminished vision, and with half his face paralyzed. After suffering this triple blow, he recovered from this devastating period in his life, and he found his way back to professional tennis, to the very height of the profession.

- Kim Clijsters, a young Belgian woman, followed her heart back to the game of tennis. She thought her tennis career might be over when doctors told her she might not play again because of a wrist injury. But, she didn't say good by to tennis. She gathered the will, the drive and the determination it took, to not only play again, she won her first Grand Slam victory at the 2005 Tennis U.S. Open. She became the first to take home the richest prize money in women's sports, $2.2 million.

What could happen to you if you let your heart lead you to tennis? Your story may not be as dramatic as those depicted here. You may just want to "play" tennis. So, follow your heart to the game.

The Real Meaning Of Tennis

So much about tennis correlates to the meaning of life. The game is physical, played with strength and psychological strategy, which of course, all help when you want to be a winner in life, as well.

Scoring begins with "love," an absolutely necessary component to the meaning of life. The social aspect of the game and good sportsmanship, are instrumental in tennis, as well as in a productive life. And, playing the sport is like taking a magic carpet ride to mobility, strength and fitness, which are all added bonuses to living a long and active life. Playing tennis challenges you to be a winner, to think aggressively, and to act quickly. Who doesn't want these qualities? All these factors work to allow you to look and feel better, too.

Another marvelous factor about tennis is that it's so spectacular, many different types of people come together to participate in the sport, both as players and as spectators. My visit to the 2006 Tennis U.S. Open, the largest annual sporting event in the nation, was empirical evidence of the popularly of tennis around the world. As I was sitting in Arthur Ashe stadium, in what seemed like, a sea of people from all over the world, despite differences in language, culture, politics, economic status, age and even physical make up, I appreciated the diversity, yet, I also knew we had one thing in common, tennis. Tennis was our common denominator. Players and spectators from across the nation, who might not otherwise ever come into contact with each other, were enjoying this sport, together.

Wherever the game is played, whether on the hard courts at the Tennis U.S. Open in New York City, on the red clay at the Foro Italico in Rome, or the lush green lawn tennis courts at Wimbledon; whether at a community park tennis court, or at an expensive tennis club, the real meaning of the game of tennis is metaphoric to the real meaning of life. Both, usually take hard work, excellence, strategic planning, wellness, love, and some enjoyment. All of which, contribute to winning quality and prosperity in our individual lives, as well as, what we work on in this world, together, as a team. The real meaning of tennis is about always finding a better, more strategic way to win.

Psychological Reasons/Advantages to Playing Tennis:

- Helps relieve tension in the player.

- Develops mental toughness and help keep the mind sharp because you work to respond quickly in tennis, and you have to recover from a point quickly. A player must easily leave behind whatever previously occurred, using strategy and intensity during the 20 to 30 seconds between points to work to stay one step ahead of the opponent.

- Develops a better work ethic, because discipline and practice is necessary to manage the fundamentals and keep mistakes at a minimum.

- One-on-one competition builds courage.

- Formulates a winning attitude and exercises good sportsmanship qualities.

- Builds integrity when making line calls.

- Attributes responsibility when serving, or playing with partners.

- Helps players be aggressive to win.

- Discipline aids a player in effectively managing stress.

- Helps in managing adversity by learning to adjust quickly.

- It's necessary to plan and implement strategies to win.

- Helps in implementing effective performance rituals, such as those done before serving, which could transfer to taking exams, conducing a meeting, giving a speech, or in giving an opening or closing argument in Court.

- Builds social skills through interaction with other players.

- Makes it easy to simply "let go" and have fun.

Physical Reasons/Advantages to Playing Tennis

- Helps coordination and balance.

- Better flexibility.

- Leg strength increases and leg muscles build and become stronger because of hundreds of starts and stops.

- Offers physical cross-training.

- Helps better recognition of nutritional habits for better results during challenging play.

- Builds bone muscle strength and density.

- Induces aerobic fitness.

Poems

Tennis Has A Rhythm!

Dance with it. Bounce with it.
Put one arm straight out and just rock with it.
Swing with it; throw some hip into it,
Dip with it and catch a drop shot with it.
Move loose, shuffle with it,
Groove with it. Adjust with it,
Oopps! I cussed with it.
Don't just play with that volley.
Clip the base line,
Cause they'll return the ball fast,
Can't just loddy doddy.
So, choose a partner, and flow with it,
Go for what you know with it,
Maybe even rock and roll with it.
Bend with it. Stretch with it, hop with it,
Twist and shout,
Work it out.
Don't ever doubt,
That the game has got ...
A rhythm.
You might as well surrender to it, be wise,
Master it, and realize ... that to it,
There's a definitive rhythm.
Something like your heartbeat,
With a musical, mystical energy,
Sometimes, like B. B. King and Lucille,
Then sometimes it's like ... violins,
Makes everything else be still.
Sometimes, like the sounds of Motown, or an operatic virtuoso.
Then other times, a smooth jazz combo, Salsa, Country and Western,
Or a choir singing gos ... pel.
Even the birds which fly by, high in the sky,
Synchronize.

Makes you wonder if they, might sometimes,
Look down and take your side.
Because you're in a sensational rhythm.
Just like you,
Tennis, too,
Has a rhythm.

Breaking News

We interrupt our regular scheduled programming for this Breaking News.
We have a developing story of how you can stay fit and have better health,
If you choose.
Thousands of Americans, Russians, Hungarians, Chinese, Africans, and
others from around the world,
are rushing to tennis courts … men, women, boys and girls.
There's been resurgence in tennis.
This could be the remedy …
Here's more now with this story. Let's see.
Turn's out, we could be on our way …
That's if more people are really committed to play,
Yes, ladies and gentlemen, tennis is on the rise.
Get ready, for miracles of anti-aging and longer lives.
It looks as if people are elated
Because tennis rackets and tennis balls are being donated,
From small businesses and large corporations.
To the less fortunate across the nation.
Churches and corporations have agreed,
Tennis benefits us all,
It's just what we need.
Tennis is a fun sport, and it's been proven,
That's why even people in wheel chairs are moving.
Keeping fit, and reducing stress,
Talk about multi-tasking! With just a friendly game of tennis.
Around the world, violence has ceased, thanks to negotiations,
During a tennis match, between leaders of two top political nations.
Yes. Good will has been announced.
And, worldwide peace could be imminent.
Simply by providing more tennis equipment.
Who ever heard of a good sportsman-like terrorist?
Tennis balls and tennis rackets have virtually put gunfire to rest.
So, might more tennis promote better health, stop political jargon and war
rivalries?

Stay close to the sport, and remain updated,
For what could turn out to be a reality.

Obsession Session

I thought I might be loosing it. You know ... a little off.
Went to see a doctor with an office in a loft.
She said, "come in, it's great to see you."
I said, "it's great to see you, too."
I was ready to confess, I'm starting to feel a little blue.
I sat on her fancy couch. It had a hidden golf ball,
I jumped up, hollered "ouch," and threw it to the wall.
It was then, I noticed golf clubs and golf balls lined the corners of the
office floor.
All the time, I was still rubbing my backside,
That golf ball made it sore!
"Can we talk?" I said.
"Go right ahead."
Then, she scribbled something down.
I sat back, relaxed, and then, began to frown.
Then, I exclaimed, "Quite honestly,
It's tennis! I've been playing a lot lately."
"So, Ms. Lady, you think you're obsessed?" She said.
Whatever you do, enjoy your life, and be sure to do your best!"
I knew she was right. Why worry about a tennis obsession?
All I had to do was look at her, if I wanted to learn a lesson!
Forget about me. She was surely a "tell-tell" sign,
Of someone having an awful lot of *golf* on their mind?
So go ahead, pursue your passion, don't think about being obsessed.
Do what makes you happy. It's worrying about it which makes you a mess!

Play Tennis

Leave your computer for the rest of the day.
Turn off your TV, and come out and play.
Grab a tennis racket; take a walk to the courts.
Get comfortable and sporty. Put on your favorite shorts.
Head to the park to get a new view,
Bring a fresh can of tennis balls,
You showboat, you!
Take time now, don't procrastinate.
You won't miss your TV, once you start feeling great!
When you go back home, you'll feel brand new.
You're likely to make new friends, too!

"Murder That Ball"

A nice lady once told me,
And she held back the nicety,
"You could have murdered that ball."
I looked at my racket, and thought,
In essence, she's telling me, "I'm not giving tennis my all."
I respected her belief in me,
To have the ability,
Her faith I did admire.
I couldn't let this go; I felt the need to show,
I really did have the desire.
"I'll show her, next time ... I bet.
Just how I can do that!"
She made a good call, after all.
So, next time, I went for the challenge, focused to put the ball away,
And, waited for the chance to murder the ball.
I gave it a try,
With my instincts,
I relied,
Because the opportunity doesn't happen every day.
I anticipated, yet, I was real low key,
Then, when I got the opportunity,
I went for the jugular, I didn't stall.
I ran up to the net, and I did it, I murdered that ball.

It Would Make A Difference

What if your job or church had a tennis league?
There would be a difference in attitudes, you would see.
What if more high schools had tennis courts and tennis programs?
Might see brilliant scores when teenagers take exams.
You see, playing tennis can help a shy person better deal with conducting a meeting.
Even, give a speech or presentation with a smile.
Could even help a lawyer build their confidence,
When giving an opening or closing argument at a jury trial.
The pressure of winning and losing on the tennis court, even increases the capacity,
To effectively deal with, and accommodate life when things can get a little nasty.
Because just like in life,
A tennis player learns to make adjustments, stay positive and win,
Even to their opponent, a smile and handshake they will lend.
Direct results … I'm sure there would be,
A world of more prosperity.

One Day I Found Tennis

One day I found tennis.
My life's a delight.
One day I found tennis.
Hey, I must have done something right.

On Watching Men Play Tennis (Those Men's' Legs)

Your legs speak their own language,
As you walk my way.
You don't know I'm looking,
But you're making my day.
Men, whose legs are more muscular than most,
Men, who could if they wanted to, yet don't need to boast.
Looking at you from afar,
Makes *me* appreciate how blessed *you* are.
The angles, the curves,
I know, I have nerve.
But, women check out men, too.
Just the way I'm checking out you.
While I'm waiting on my next game, you've got me sitting on edge,
I think I'm in love with you, because your legs.
Hey! What's your name?
Before my next game!
Nothing serious, just shooting the breeze.
All because you look athletic and gentlemanly,
and you're such a tease.
Yeh, this game is just the right sport,
To check out the men's legs in their sporty tennis shorts.

Imagine This World ...

If more people played tennis.
Just how different would this world be?
Just imagine if everyone played tennis, just one day a week.
Monumental achievements would happen,
Because of networking and forming more camaraderie.
All, while we "played" our tennis game,
We just kept getting more fit.
Imagine that! Just because we enjoyed doing it!

Conclusion

No matter how spectacular you look, genetics can take you only so far. That's why I'm so impressed with the game of tennis. It's got everything you need to live longer and look your best, all packed into a fun, and social sport.

Compared to other major sports, tennis is relatively overlooked and understated. I had never thought about playing tennis as an option to routine workouts. Thank God, I met someone to take me to a sport I may have otherwise ignored. You can have so much fun, and feel so fit and healthy when you participate in tennis, that you're motivated to work out more often. The social atmosphere for meeting new people, and staying in touch with others, who participate in the sport, can be incredibly fun. And, the diversity of people you can meet is almost endless. You have the opportunity to play tennis with inspiring and remarkable people at any tennis court.

The sport of tennis is alive, yet dormant in many communities, when more people of all ages, races, and cultures can benefit from the advantages this sport offers, both as a recreational, as well as, a spectator sport. Many high schools don't have tennis teams and tennis courts. Many cities have neighborhoods with poorly manicured tennis courts, even when the rest of the park is well maintained. Admittedly, tennis lessons and court time can sometimes be expensive. Tennis rackets and tennis shoes can sometimes get costly. Nonetheless, the game of tennis should be promoted more and advanced, in every arena of society, especially in multi-cultural areas, by all effective means.

You see, I have an outlook about tennis, as a "cure all" to obesity, high blood pressure, stress, boredom, depression, hyperactivity, violence and so much more.

Since the day I found tennis, the passion I have developed for the game, for what tennis offers, and for the people I meet along this journey of thrills and excitement, have all made me a fan for life. I look forward to *everyone* else being fans of tennis, too!

Glossary Of Tennis Terms For Your Tennis Game

A

- Ace—A good serve that is un-returnable and not touched.

- Ad court—The side of the court in which the second point of each game begins. Also called the left court or backhand court.

- Advantage—The game point following deuce. If a player wins the "advantage" point, he or she wins the game.

- Alley—The area on each side of the singles court that enlarges the surface area for doubles play.

- All-rounder—A player with the ability to play well both offensively and defensively.

- Approach shot—A shot used from inside the baseline to enable a player at or near the baseline on the opposite side of the court to attain position at the net.

- Australian doubles formation—A serving formation in doubles wherein the server and server's partner is initially positioned on the same side of the court.

- Australian grip—A grip midway between the Eastern and Continental, so named because it was developed in Australia to facilitate serve-and-volley play on grass.

B

- **Backhand**—For a right-hander, the stroke played on the left side of the body; the reverse for a left-hander.

- **Backspin or under spin**—the reverse or backward rotation of the ball in flight.

- **Back swing**—The initial portion of the swing, so called because it involves bringing the racket back before swinging it forward. It can be straight back or loop.

- **Ball toss**—The action of tossing the ball into the air with the non-racket arm when initiating the serve.

- **Baseline**—The line which demarcates the legal length of the court.

- **Best of three (or five)**—Refers to the maximum number of sets in any match. In "best of three" matches, players need to win two of the three sets. In men's tennis, matches can be "best of five," i.e.; a match finishes when a player has won three sets.

- **Break (of service)**—Where the serving player loses the game.

- **Block volley**—A volley produced by holding the racket firmly in the path of the oncoming ball and "blocking" it back with almost no motion.

- **Bye**—Free passage into the second round of a tournament. Players may be given a bye if a tournament doesn't have enough players (e.g. if there are only 28 players in a tournament designed for 32, there will be 4 byes in the first round). Byes are awarded to seeded players.

C

- **Centerline**—Refers to both the line dividing the service boxes and the smaller hash mark that bisects the baseline.

- Changeover—the time after every odd game when players change ends of the court; they have 90 seconds to make the changeover.

- Chip shot—a soft dipping shot with backspin that just clears the net, forcing the net player to volley up; often employed to return serve.

- Chop shot—A stroke with heavy backspin, hit with a chopping motion.

- Circular back swing or loop back swing—Taking the racket back in a high, looping or circular motion.

- Clay court—A court with a surface made of rushed shale, stone or brick. It can be red or green. The French Open is played on clay.

- Closed face.—When the face of the racket is inclined slightly forward, tilted toward the oncoming ball.

- Contact point—The place where and when the racket meets the ball.

- Continental grip—A grip which is the same for forehand and backhand, so called because it was developed on the "continent" of Europe; favored by serve-and-volley players.

- Crosscourt shot—A ball hit diagonally across the court, as opposed to one hit straight down the line.

- Cross slice—A shot hit with under spin, or backspin, and sidespin at the same time.

D

- Defensive lob—A high, deep lob played from a defensive position which allows the defender time to recover position and forces the offensive player away from the net: almost always hit with under spin.

- Deuce—The score in a game where both players have forty points.

- Deuce court—The side of the court in which the first point of each game begins. Also called the right court or the forehand court.

- Dink shot—A soft dipping shot that just clears the net, used often in doubles, especially on return of serve.

- Double fault—Failing to place either of two serves in play.

- Drag volley—A volley hit with the racket face slightly open, producing some backspin; used for control.

- Drive volley or swing volley—Playing the ball in the air with longer swing than the normal short volley movement.

- Drop shot—A delicate shot that barely clears the net and falls short in the opponents court.

- Drop volley—Same as the drop shot, but hit off a volley, usually from a position close to the net.

E

- Eastern grip—a strong ground stroking grip, so called because it was developed in the eastern United States, that employs separate hand positions for forehand and backhand.

- Exhibition matches—Matches arranged outside official competitions as a form of public entertainment. Those matches are not sanctioned by the Tours.

F

- Fast courts—Court surfaces such as asphalt and concrete.

- Flat back swing—Taking the racket straight back in preparation for the swing, as opposed to a loop or circular back swing.

- Flat face—When the strings of the racket are perpendicular to the ground and the racket meets the ball squarely, with little spin.

- Flat serve—A serve hit with little or no spin; usually it is hit with great speed and power.

- Flat shot—Any shot hit with little or no spin, usually it is hit with great speed and power.

- Follow through—The finishing motion of the swing after the ball has been hit.

- Foot fault—An error occurring when a player steps onto or over the baseline, sideline or the center mark when serving.

- Footwork—A player's technique for moving most economically to the ideal position to play a stroke. Techniques include tango, side step and cross-step.

- Forcing shot—Any shot that forces one's opponent into a defensive position.

- Forehand—For a right-handed person, the stroke played on the right side of the body; opposite for a left handed person

G

- Game—Part of a set. Every set consists of at least six games.

- Ground stroke—Hitting the ball after it has bounced, usually from the area of the baseline.

- Ground stroke slice—A ground stroke hit with an open-faced racket producing backspin or under spin.

- Gut—A responsive string, made from animal intestines, used to string rackets.

H

- Half court—The area of the court midway between the baseline and net. Also called mid-court.

- Half-volley—Playing the ball just after it bounces with a very low, short stroke.

- Hard or composition courts—A court surface that is hard to the touch and on the feet.

- Hard court—A tennis court with a surface made out of asphalt, concrete or a similar material. The U.S. Open and the Australian Open are played on hard courts.

- Head—the area of the racket containing the strings.

- Hitting on the rise—Playing the ball before it has reached the peak of its bounce. Also known as "taking the ball early."

K

- Kick serve—A serve with heavy spin, causing it to change direction or bounce unexpectedly when it lands in the service court. Also known as a twist serve.

- Kill—To "put the ball away" and end the point.

- Knockout competition—A tournament whereby players are eliminated when they lose a match. Most events are played with this format, except for the Masters, the Hopman Cup or the Fed Cup.

L

- Let—An invalid point, which has to be replayed. Occurs when a serve touches the net but still lands in the correct service court.

- Line judge—Line judges have the task of deciding whether a ball has landed in the court or outside. The umpire can only overrule their decisions.

- Lob—A high-arcing shot, usually hit from behind the baseline to regain position.

- Long line—A stroke played straight down the court, either along or adjacent to one of the sidelines.

- Love—Zero in tennis language. Love-thirty is 0-30.

- Lucky Loser—In some knockout tournaments one defeat does not automatically result in elimination. Beaten players have the chance to play again, if for instance a player withdrew. These players are known as "lucky losers."

M

- Mid-court—The area around the service lines, halfway between the net and the baseline.

- Mini-break—When the server loses the point during a tiebreak, this is referred to a mini-break.

- Mixed doubles—A match involving two teams, each team consisting of one male and one female.

- Moon ball. A very high lob, primarily to change the tempo.

N

- Net or Let—The call from the net-cord judge when a serve touches the top of the net.

- Net player—In doubles, the partner of the server when he or she takes a normal doubles position at the net.

- Net rusher—A player who aggressively moves forward to a position at the net.

- "No-man's" land—The area between the baseline the service line.

- No up—The call from the umpire when a ball having bounced twice, is dead.

O

- **Offensive lob**—A lob played from an intermediate or offensive position, usually hit with a lower trajectory than the defensive lob, and intended to win the point, often hit with topspin.

- **Open face**—When the face of the racket is tilted away from the oncoming ball, or "open" the ball, as opposed to "closed."

- **Open stance**—Any hitting stance in which the back foot is closer to the path of the ball than the front foot.

- **Overhead smash**—A stroke played above the head with a service-type action, usually from near the net and in response to a lob.

P

- **Passing shot**—A ground stroke that passes a net player on either side.

- **Penalty points**—Points deducted for unsporting behavior.

- **Placement**—Placing a shot so that it cannot be returned.

- **Punch volley**—A volley marked by a very short "punching" movement of the racket.

- **Put-away volley**—A volley hit beyond the opponent's reach.

Q

- **Qualifying competition**—Tournament giving low-ranked players the opportunity to qualify for the main draw.

R

- **Rally**—Play exchange between two or more players.

- **Ready position**—A preparation for any shot; weight slightly forward, knees slightly bent, racket up and in front of the body.

- Run-around forehand—A forehand hit from the backhand side, i.e., a player runs to his or her backhand side in order to hit a forehand instead of a backhand.

S

- Second serve—When serving, players have two chances to hit the ball in the opponent's service court. If the first attempt fails, they receive a "second serve."

- Seeding—A graded list of the best players entering a tournament. The best players are normally "seeded" before a tournament begins. This prevents these players from being drawn against each other and knocking each other out during the early rounds of the competition.

- Semi-continental—A combination of the forehand and backhand grips. This grip can be used for most shots, but particularly for volleys, serves and smashes.

- Semi-Western grip—A grip midway between the Western and Eastern grips.

- Serve or Service—Every point begins with a serve. From a position behind the baseline, the server has to hit the ball diagonally over the net into the opponent's service court. Players get two attempts to serve the ball correctly for each point. In the first point of any game or set, the serve is played from the right-hand side of the court. After this, the server alternates sides (from right to left and vice-versa) at the start of every new point.

- Serve-and-volley—A style of play that involves rushing toward the net immediately after the serve in order to volley the return.

- Service box—the area on the other side of the net in which a serve must land in order to be legal.

- Service break—when one player wins a game while the other player is serving; also called "a break."

- Service line—The line near mid-court that marks the boundaries of the service boxes.

- Set—A unit of scoring; the first player to win six games by a margin of two (or win a special tiebreak game of 6-6) wins a set.

- Side slice—Moving the racket across and under the ball at impact, imparting both backspin and sidespin at the same time, also called sidespin.

- Sidespin—Spin which causes the ball to rotate horizontally.

- Sideways stance—Standing in neither a closed nor an open stance; also referred to as a "square" stance.

- Slice—A slice shot differs from a "drive" in that the backspin applied keeps it in the air for longer, causing it to travel farther before bouncing.

- Slow courts—Courts that grab the ball on impact, slowing the bounce.

- Snap volley—A volley hit with some wrist action at impact, used for more power.

- Soft courts—Courts that give under the feet, i.e., clay.

- Specialty shots—Shots other than the basic serve, volley, and ground strokes, i.e., drop shot, approach, half-volley, lob and overhead.

- Stand in—When the receiver stands inside the baseline to return serve, intending to play the ball early.

- Standard doubles formation—Positions for the serving team, server stands at baseline with partner at net; for the receiving team, receiver stands near the baseline with partner on the service line.

- Stringing—The elasticity of the strings depends on the tension with which the racquet is strung. In general, gut strings are more elastic than synthetic strings, as a result of which they are generally strung more tautly. Players who like to hit the ball fast and hard usually prefer tauter strings. Touch players, by contrast, tend to prefer slightly slacker stringing.

- Stop volley—A volley where the player takes the pace off the ball, so that it drops softly on the other side of the net—making it difficult or impossible for the opponent to reach.

T

- "T" The mid-court area formed by the junction of the center service line and the service lines.

- Taking the net—Moving from the baseline position to the net position.

- Tennis elbow—Pain in the elbow caused by too much play, improper technique, improper tension or any combination of the three.

- Tension—The degree of tautness in the strings of a racket.

- Tie breaker or Tiebreak—A special game played to decide the winner of a set when the score is tied at 6-6. The winner of the tie breaker game is the first player to reach seven points by a margin of two.

- Top spin—Forward rotation of the ball in flight.

- Twist serve—A service played with topspin and sidespin. The ball bounces awkwardly sideways and upwards from the service court.

U

- Umpire—The umpire decides which player has won a point and also keeps the score. In major tournaments the umpire is assisted by a number of judges (e.g. line judges).

- Unforced error—An error made while under no pressure from the opponent.

V

- Vertical face—When the hitting area of the racket is at a right angle to the ground or "on edge," as opposed to open or a closed face.

- Volley—Playing the ball in the air before the ball bounces.

W

- Walkover—A win without playing because one of the players withdrew before the match started.

- Western grip—A grip developed on hard courts in California, allowing a player to hit high-bouncing balls with power and promoting topspin.

- Wildcard—Irrespective of their positions in the rankings, an organizer can invite one or more players to take part in a tournament, offering the wildcards. This gives event organizers the opportunity of offering places to promising young players, or alternatively to stars who have failed to register in time for the tournament.

- Winner—A ball hit beyond the opponent's reach; an un-returnable shot.

References

Follow Your Heart To Tennis (excerpts taken from) Tennis—Wikipedia http://en.wikipedia.org/wiki/Tennis 1. "Black History Biographies—Serena Williams."

http://www.galegroup.com/free_resources/bhm/williams_s.html. (accessed 1/23/07).

2. Garber, Greg. TENNIS—Garber: More than a tennis player. "Ashe's Activism Help Mold The Future."

http://espn.go.com/tennis/s/2003/0205/1504540.html. (accessed 8/26/05).

3. "Althea Gibson, First African-American to Win Wimbledon, Florida A & M University Multi-Sports Star."

http://www.thesiac.com/person/altheagibson.inc. (accessed 10/6/05).

4. United States Tennis Association. "Navratilova Helps Kick Off Tennis Month."

http://www.usta.com/news/fullstory.sps?iType=841& inewsid=326740 (accessed 5/2/06).

5. Tennis Tournament Betting. "Age-defying Agassi Marches On to Face Come Backing Blake."

http://tennis-betting.blogspot.com/2005/09/age-defying-agassi-marches-on-to-face.html. (accessed 5/5/06)

6. Associated Press, <u>Tennis</u>. "Kim Clijsters Powers Past Pierce For U.S. Open Crown."

http://www.ustatoday.com/sports/tennis/open/2005-09-10-womens-final_x.html. (accessed) 5/5/06).

Glossary Of Tennis Terms For Your Tennis Game. <u>Tennis</u>. "Tennis Terminology."

http://www.sportsline.com/tennis/story/6145343. (accessed 11/15/06).

Tennis Connections

- Cardio Tennis—Check out USTA.com for aerobic/tennis fitness.

- Tennis Welcome Center.com.—Enter your zip code and find the nearest tennis center near you to go out and play. It's an easy way to look for a new place to play and new competition.

- Visit USTA.com.—United States Tennis Association is the national governing body for the sport of tennis. USTA is the largest tennis organization in the world and this organization has a professional staff dedicated to growing the game.

- TENNIS, the magazine, published three times year, is a comprehensive way to learn about the game.

978-0-595-43647-7
0-595-43647-1